KB244180

Restless Earth

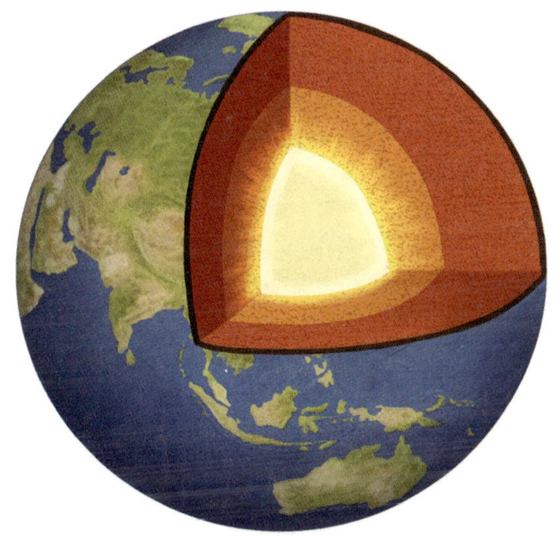

About Wise & Wide

- A systematic 6-level English reading program based on Lexile® measures
- Diverse and interesting topics chosen from the elementary curriculums of Korea and English speaking western countries
- Well-written books in various forms including fiction stories, descriptive texts, and classics retold
- The informative but original fiction stories grab your interest, leading to the easy and clear understanding of the educational content.
- Improve thinking skills with solid after-reading activities at all levels of the series.

Wise & Wide is a 6-level English reading program that consists of 60 books and each level is systematically divided by Lexile® measures. The Lexile® Framework for Reading is the most popular reading measuring system in American formal education curriculums and many English programs. Over 20 out of 50 states in the U.S. mark Lexile® measures directly on students' final report cards and over 300 well-known publishers adopt and use Lexile® measures.

Experience many kinds of readings written by professional writers from the U.S. and England. They used interesting topics that were carefully chosen after analyzing elementary curriculums from around the world including Korea, the U.S., England, and Australia among many others. Comprehensive after-reading activities including graphic organizers, speaking tasks, and After-reading Tests are ready for you.

Levels in the series and their corresponding Lexile® measures

Level	Lexile® measures	U.S. Grade
Level 1	Below 200L	Pre K - K
Level 2	190L - 400L	Lower Grade 1
Level 3	350L - 530L	Upper Grade 1
Level 4	420L - 650L	Grade 2
Level 5	520L - 940L	Grade 3 - 4
Level 6	830L - 1070L	Grade 5 - 6

* Smart Readers: Wise & Wide level 1 is applicable to the preschool level in the U.S.
* The source of the relationship between Lexile® measures and U.S. school grades: CCSS(Common Core State Standards) FOR ENGLISH LANGUAGE ARTS, APPENDIX A (2012, which is used by 45 states in the U.S.)

Topic List

	Level 1	Level 2	Level 3	Level 4	Level 5	Level 6
Book 1	Science>Biology: The hibernation of animals Story	Science>Biology: Living and nonliving things Story	Science>Biology> Animals & the Environment: Sea otters Story	Environment> Living with nature: The diver & the persimmon tree Story	Science>Biology> Animal: Amazing animals of the Amazon Story	Science>Biology: Germs, transmitted diseases Story
Book 2	Literature> World classics: Aesop's fables Story	Literature> Traditional fairy tale: Old tales about stones Story	Social Studies> Economy: To run a business to make and save money Story	Science>Biology> Plants: Photosynthesis Story	Science>Earth science: Earth's layers, earthquakes, volcanoes, and earth's atmosphere Report	Mathematics> Sequence: The golden ratio & the Fibonacci sequence Story
Book 3	Science>Physics: How shadows are formed Story	Literature> World classics: Peter Pan Story	Science>Scientific technology: Nanobots Story	Literature>Myths: World's creation stories Story	Literature> Legend: The story of King Arthur Story	
Book 4	Literature> Traditional literature: The Talmud Story	Science>Biology> Animal: Polar bears Story	Science>Biology> Animal: Mountain gorillas Story	Social Studies> Cultural anthropology: Amazing ancient cultures of the world Story	Science> Earth science: Clouds and weather Story	
Book 5			Social Studies> Cultural anthropology: Astonishing festivals Report	Art>Music: Stories from two operas Story		
Book 6				Social Studies> People: Three great people who overcame hardships Story		
Book 7						
Book 8						
Book 9						
Book 10						

* 10 books in each level will be published.

How to Use This Book

•Before Reading

You can easily find the topic and what kind of story you are about to read.

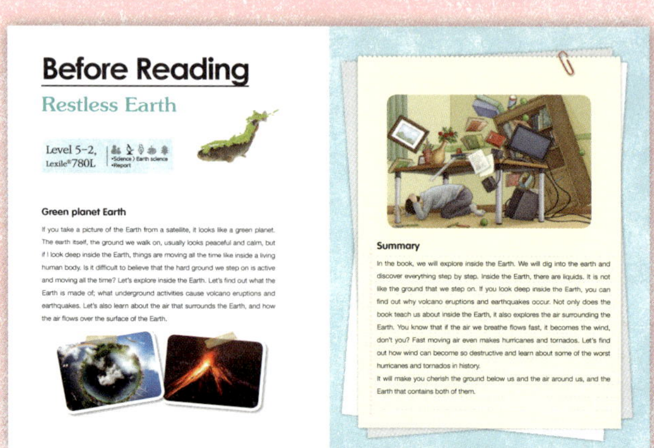

•The text

All the stories were written by professional writers from the U.S. and England, so you will read authentic and appropriate English sentences and expressions in every book in the series.

•Pop Quiz

Check out right away if you understand what you have just read by solving a pop quiz that checks your comprehension.

•Key Words

The key words and expressions on each page are listed for you to easily study them.

•Aha! Tips

Download free Korean explanations at *www.ihappyhouse.co.kr* for all of the sentences marked with "Aha!". These explain cultural, scientific, and economic knowledge or they deal with aspects of English such as grammatical structures or idiomatic expressions. There are lots of "Aha! Tips" to help you understand the text.

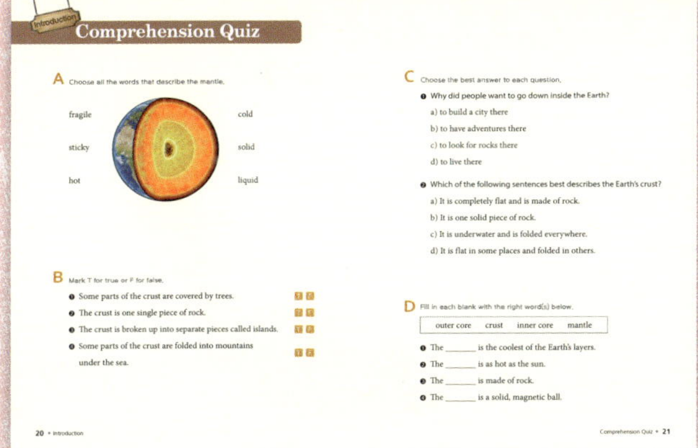

•Comprehension Quiz

After reading one chapter, solve various questions to find out if you fully understand the content.

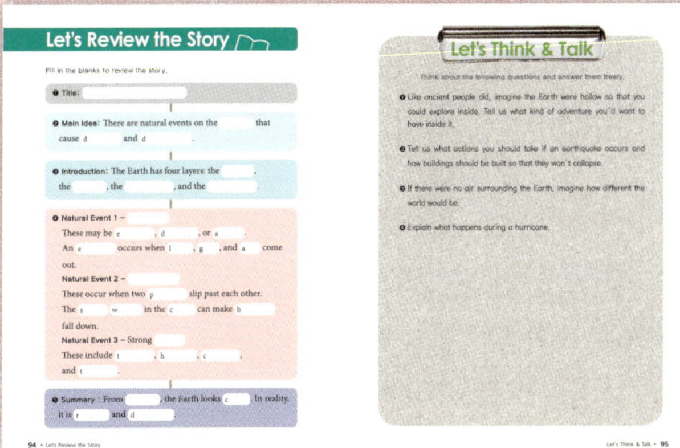

•Let's Review the Story /
•Let's Think & Talk

Fill in the blanks in the organizer to summarize the whole story. Express your own thinking and feelings about the story by answering the questions. You can build up logic and reasoning skills for your essay examinations in the future.

Appendix

Audio CD
In the CD audio book form, the texts are read vividly by American professional voice actors.

After-reading Test
Solve an additionally provided After-reading Test for each book.

The Korean translation, Answer Keys, a Word Quiz, a Word List, and Aha! Tips for each book
You can download them for free at *www.ihappyhouse.co.kr*

Before Reading

Restless Earth

Level 5-2,
Lexile® 780L

• Science › Earth science
• Report

Green planet Earth

If you take a picture of the Earth from a satellite, it looks like a green planet. The earth itself, the ground we walk on, usually looks peaceful and calm, but if I look deep inside the Earth, things are moving all the time like inside a living human body. Is it difficult to believe that the hard ground we step on is active and moving all the time? Let's explore inside the Earth. Let's find out what the Earth is made of; what underground activities cause volcano eruptions and earthquakes. Let's also learn about the air that surrounds the Earth, and how the air flows over the surface of the Earth.

Summary

In the book, we will explore inside the Earth. We will dig into the earth and discover everything step by step. Inside the Earth, there are liquids. It is not like the ground that we step on. If you look deep inside the Earth, you can find out why volcano eruptions and earthquakes occur. Not only does the book teach us about inside the Earth, it also explores the air surrounding the Earth. You know that if the air we breathe flows fast, it becomes the wind, don't you? Fast moving air even makes hurricanes and tornados. Let's find out how wind can become so destructive and learn about some of the worst hurricanes and tornados in history.

It will make you cherish the ground below us and the air around us, and the Earth that contains both of them.

Contents

Restless Earth

2   About Wise & Wide
4   How to Use This Book
6   Before Reading

Introduction
10   Dig Down Deep
20   Comprehension Quiz

Chapter One
22   Violent Volcanoes
36   Comprehension Quiz

Chapter Two
38   The Science of Volcanoes
50   Comprehension Quiz

Chapter Three
52   Shaking All Over
74   Comprehension Quiz

Chapter Four
76   Up in the Air
92   Comprehension Quiz

94   Let's Review the Story
95   Let's Think & Talk
96   Let's Review the Story (Answers)
97   After-reading Test

Restless Earth

Dig Down Deep

Over hundreds of years, different people have had different ideas about the Earth. Some people believed that the Earth floated in space like a big island. They thought that it hung from four ropes fastened to the sky. Others believed that the Earth was a flat plate balancing on the back of a tortoise.

KEY WORDS

- **dig** (dig-dug-dug)
- **over**
- **float**
- **in space**
- **hang** (hang-hung-hung)
- **fasten**
- **flat**
- **plate**
- **balance**

Many wondered if the Earth was hollow and hoped that people could go down and have adventures inside it.

In 1972, astronauts took a photograph that amazed the world. It was the first ever picture of the entire planet Earth. For the first time, ordinary people could see what their planet looked like. It looked like a sparkling blue and white jewel hanging in space. It looked fragile and beautiful—a peaceful place to live. But is it really so fragile and peaceful?

POP QUIZ

Match the two sides.

Some people believed that...

ⓐ the Earth floated in space •

ⓑ the Earth was a flat plate •

• ① on the back of a tortoise.

• ② and was hanging from four ropes.

KEY WORDS

- wonder
- hollow
- astronaut
- amaze
- the first ever
- sparkling
- fragile

Millions of earthquakes shake the ground every year. There are over a hundred volcanoes erupting at any moment. Hurricanes and violent storms swirl about the planet. We stand on the Earth, and we think it is solid, but have you ever wondered exactly what is beneath your feet?

Imagine the Earth is like an enormous onion made up of different layers. We can't peel them off, but scientists can tell us what those layers are made of. The first layer is the surface that we all live on. This is called the crust. It is made of solid rock, and it goes all the way around the Earth like the skin on an apple.

In some places it is very flat. In other places, it is folded into high mountains and deep valleys. Even under the sea, there are mountain ranges. Sometimes the tops of these mountains stick out above the water and make an island.

KEY WORDS

- at any moment
- volcano
- erupt
- violent
- swirl
- solid
- enormous
- be made up of
- layer
- peel off
- be made of
- crust
- surface
- all the way
- fold into
- stick out

Some parts of the crust are just bare rock. In other places,
the rocky crust is covered with grass, rainforest, sand, or food
crops. Most of the crust is covered by the ocean, with huge
areas called continents sticking up above the water. People
and land animals all live on the continents. They are like giant
islands.

Although the crust covers the entire Earth, it is not a solid piece
of rock. It is made of several enormous pieces that join together.
These are called plates, and they are moving all the time. 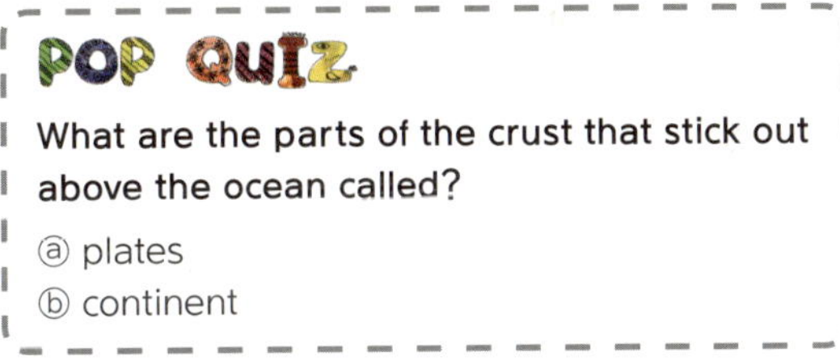

POP QUIZ

What are the parts of the crust that stick out
above the ocean called?

ⓐ plates
ⓑ continent

KEY WORDS

- bare
- rocky
- be covered with
- rainforest
- crop
- continent
- stick up
- entire
- solid
- join

But how can they move about? To answer this question, we need to know what is beneath the crust. Directly below it, there is a layer called the mantle. This layer, also made of rock, is almost 3,000 km deep and incredibly hot.

At the lower part of the mantle, it is hotter than the upper part. This causes convection currents in the mantle.

Some of the rock in this layer can be melted, and this molten rock is called magma.

The different plates of the Earth's crust float on the mantle. They are free to move about.

The convection currents near the surface slowly pull them together or force them apart. 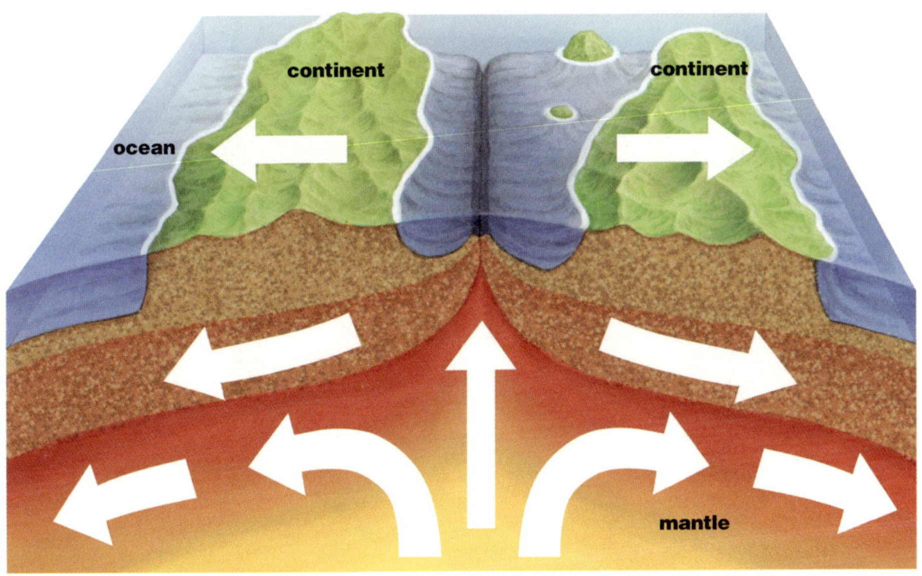

convection currents in the mantle

KEY WORDS

- mantle
- incredibly
- lower
- upper
- convection current
- melt
- molten
- magma
- be free to
- move about
- force apart

But what is beneath the mantle?

There is another layer of scorching metal called the outer core.
This layer is even hotter than the mantle although nobody has
ever measured it.

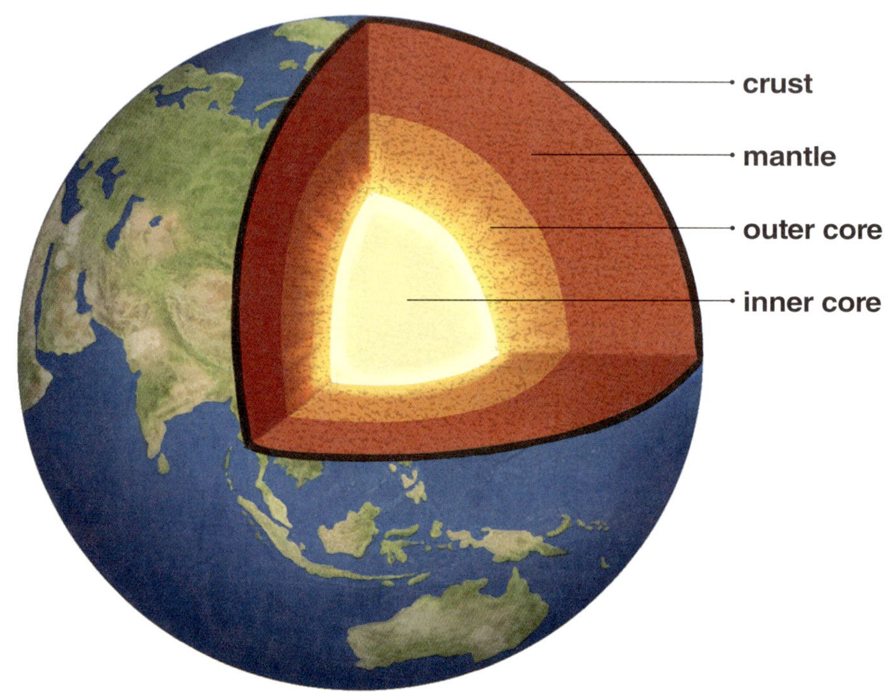

KEY WORDS

- scorching
- core
- measure
- estimate

- sticky
- weight
- press
- diameter

- extremely
- magnetic
- protect
- instantly (= at once)

Scientists have used mathematics to estimate the temperature at 4,000-6,000°C. This is about the same as the surface of the sun! This layer is much less sticky than the mantle.

At last, we come to the very center of the Earth: the inner core. This is made up of the same kinds of metals as the outer core. However, since there is so much weight pressing on it from the layers above, it is a solid ball of metal. Imagine a metal ball 2,400 km in diameter, as hot as the sun, and extremely magnetic. It is sitting there below us all the time. If we didn't have the outer layers of the Earth to protect us from its heat, we would die instantly!

POP QUIZ

Why doesn't the heat of the inner core kill all humans?

ⓐ The outer core is a cold layer that cools the inner core.
ⓑ The outer layers of the Earth protect humans from it.

Comprehension Quiz

A Choose all the words that describe the mantle.

fragile

sticky

hot

cold

solid

liquid

B Mark T for true or F for false.

1. Some parts of the crust are covered by trees. T F

2. The crust is one single piece of rock. T F

3. The crust is broken up into separate pieces called islands. T F

4. Some parts of the crust are folded into mountains under the sea. T F

C Choose the best answer to each question.

❶ Why did people want to go down inside the Earth?

    a) to build a city there

    b) to have adventures there

    c) to look for rocks there

    d) to live there

❷ Which of the following sentences best describes the Earth's crust?

    a) It is completely flat and is made of rock.

    b) It is one solid piece of rock.

    c) It is underwater and is folded everywhere.

    d) It is flat in some places and folded in others.

D Fill in each blank with the right word(s) below.

outer core	crust	inner core	mantle

❶ The __________ is the coolest of the Earth's layers.

❷ The __________ is as hot as the sun.

❸ The __________ is made of rock.

❹ The __________ is a solid, magnetic ball.

Chapter One

Violent Volcanoes

What do you think of when you hear the word “volcano”? You probably think of a cone-shaped mountain erupting with fire and smoke. This is true of some volcanoes, but there is a lot more to understand.

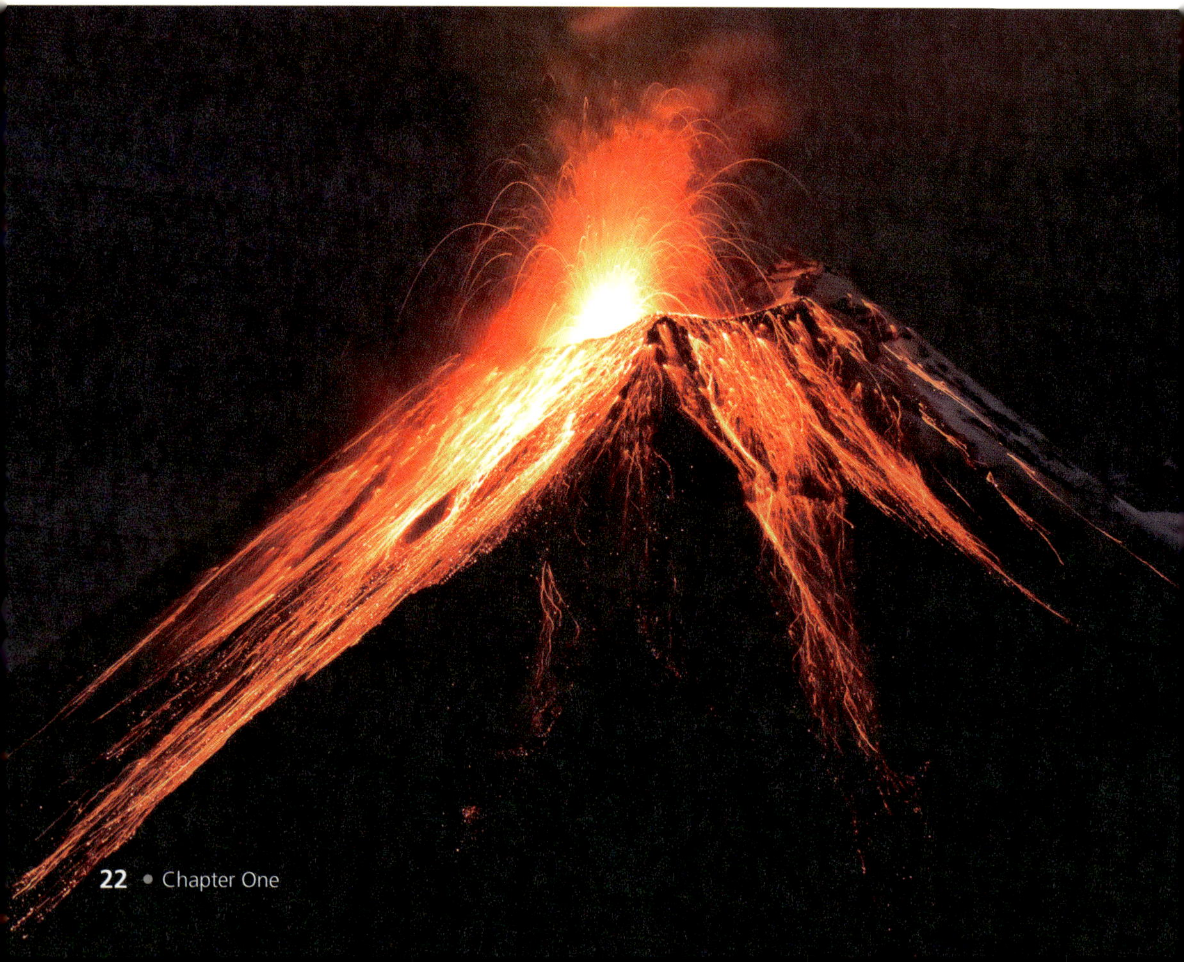

Volcanoes can have different shapes and sizes. Some erupt suddenly and violently while others quietly erupt all the time! So what exactly is a volcano? The word comes from Vulcan, the Roman god of fire. 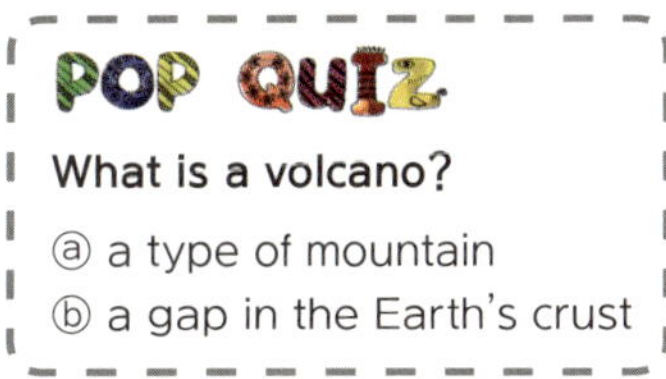 It is a gap, or vent, in the Earth's crust that lets magma through.

To explain how a volcano is formed, we need to think about the plates. Remember that they are pulled and pushed about by convection currents in the mantle.

POP QUIZ

What is a volcano?

ⓐ a type of mountain
ⓑ a gap in the Earth's crust

KEY WORDS

- cone-shaped
- come from
- gap
- vent
- let A through
- form

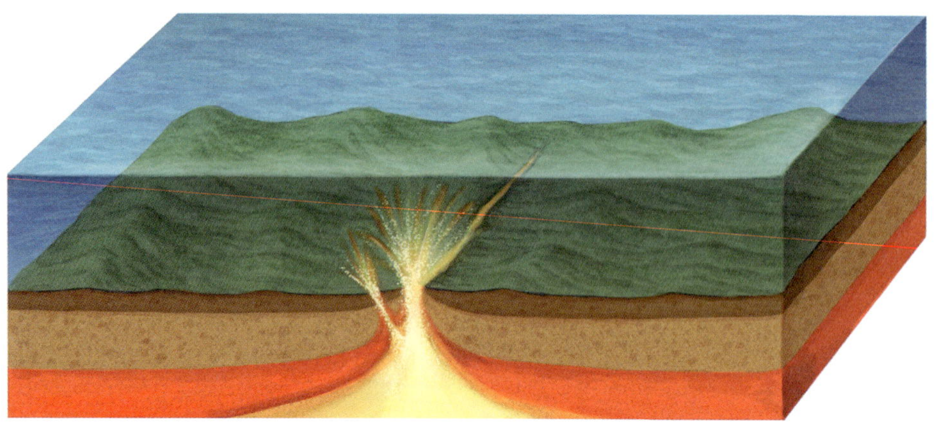

▲ If two plates are pulled apart where they met, volcanoes appear.

Where two or more plates meet, volcanoes appear. If two plates are pulled apart, a gap appears between them. Aha!

This is common under the sea, where the crust is thinner.

Magma bubbles up through the gap, hits the cold seawater, and cools to a solid.

In this way, long chains of volcanoes are formed on the seabed.

They normally erupt gently and are long, low, and thin.

KEY WORDS

- appear
- thinner
- bubble up
- seabed
- thin
- underneath
- turn into
- find one's way onto
- crack
- gather
- burst out

If two plates are pushed together, one of them may go underneath the other. That part of the crust melts and turns into magma.

The magma finds its way onto the surface through a crack. If there is not a crack, the magma begins to gather beneath the crust. It pushes upward until, at last, the magma bursts out. This is a volcanic eruption.

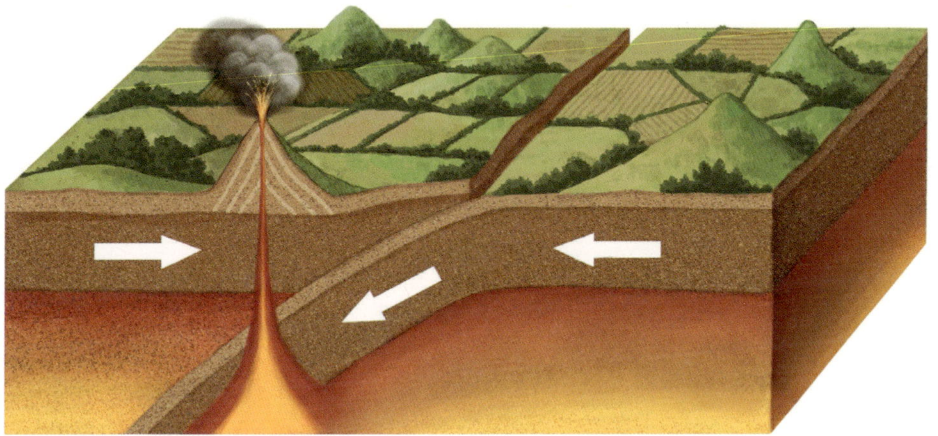

▲ If one of the two plates goes underneath the other, volcanoes appear.

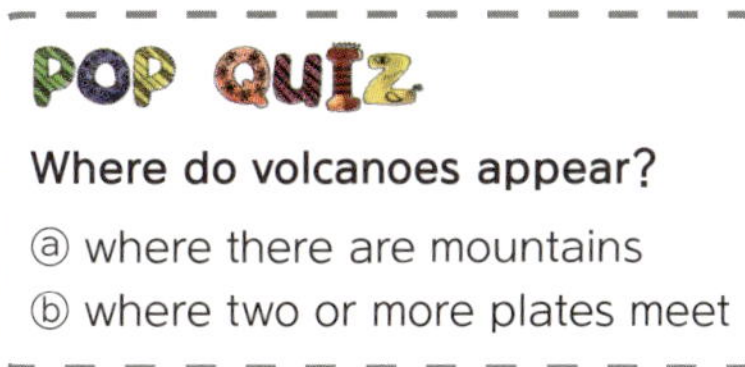

KEY WORDS
lava
depend on
thick
spiky
pour
basalt
granite
material

When magma appears on the Earth's surface, it is called lava. It moves like a river of melted rock called a lava flow.

▲ basalt

All lava is dangerous, but there are different types. The danger to human life depends on how far and fast the lava flows. Some lava is thick and moves slowly. The surface cools quite quickly and forms a hard, spiky surface. Other types of lava are thinner and less sticky. They move more quickly and pour out of volcanoes in great rivers. When the lava cools,

▲ granite

it forms rocks such as basalt and granite. Basalt is especially common beneath the sea, where the lava cools quickly. Granite is very hard, and it is often used as a building material.

POP QUIZ

Match the two sides.

ⓐ basalt •　　　•　① often used as a building material
ⓑ granite •　　　•　② common under the sea

But it is not only lava that is thrown out by an erupting volcano. Some volcanoes also send out clouds of ash and dust. The ash goes into the air and falls down onto the ground. Sometimes it falls close to the volcano and makes it difficult for people to breathe. The tiny specks of dust and rock get into their lungs. If the ash is thick enough, it blocks sunlight for a while. It forms a thick layer on cars, houses, and crops.

The ash can go higher into the air and travel to other countries. In 2010, a volcano in Iceland produced an ash cloud. It forced many airports in Europe to close. It was too dangerous to fly aircraft because the ash could get into the engines.

KEY WORDS

- **throw out** (throw-threw-thrown)
- ash
- speck
- get into
- block
- crop
- travel
- aircraft

Flashes of lightning are often seen in these ash clouds. Tiny pieces of dust and rock rub together very quickly. This makes electricity, which leaps out of the cloud as lightning. Since most people won't go near a volcano during an eruption, this is not dangerous.

However, there is something far more deadly that may happen. It is something that can kill thousands of people in seconds.

It is something so fast moving that nobody can outrun it. It is something so hot that it will instantly burn up trees, animals, and people.

It is a deadly current of hot, toxic gas, and rock. It pours down the slopes of a volcano. It may pick up large rocks and tree trunks and carry them along. It can destroy entire towns and cities.

▲ a deadly current of hot, toxic gas, and rock, which scientists call pyroclastic flow

KEY WORDS

- flash
- rub
- electricity
- leap (leap-leapt-leapt)
- deadly
- outrun
- instantly
- burn up
- toxic
- slope
- pick up
- trunk
- carry along
- destroy

In 1902, a volcano erupted on the island of Martinique. The toxic flow destroyed the capital city. 30,000 people were killed almost instantly.

▲ the ancient Roman town of Pompeii

POP QUIZ

What is a plaster cast?
ⓐ a solid model
ⓑ photograph

In 79 A.D., a similar flow of gas and rock came from Mount Vesuvius in Italy. It destroyed the Roman town of Pompeii. The flow killed all of the people and animals. Their bodies were

▲ a body covered in deep layers of ash from Mount Vesuvius in Pompeii

covered in deep layers of ash. They lay hidden for centuries until archaeologists discovered their remains. Where the bodies had been, there were hollows in the hard ash. They were the shapes of people, animals, food, and tools. The archaeologists made plaster casts of them and learned a lot about life in Roman times.

KEY WORDS

- **flow**
- **mount** (= mountain)
- **A.D.**(anno domini)
- **lie hidden** (lie-lay-lain)
- **archaeologist**
- **discover**
- **remains**
- **plaster cast**

Sometimes the stones and dirt in such a toxic flow can mix with water. They form a deadly river of mud called a lahar. You may not think that mud can be lethal, but it moves very quickly. The mud flows up to 160 km per hour, and it can be up to 140 m deep. It covers everything in its path. Vehicles and buildings are swept away. Farmland and crops are buried.

In 1991, Mount Pinatubo erupted in the Philippines. A lahar killed hundreds of people and left a million others homeless. The precious rice fields were destroyed. People had no way to earn a living. The mud buried entire cities, and there is still a lot of ash on the slopes of the volcano. Aha!

KEY WORDS

- dirt
- lahar
- lethal (= deadly)
- up to
- path
- sweep away (sweep-swept-swept)
- homeless
- earn a living
- bury

When there is heavy rain, this ash turns into mud and begins to flow again. Even now, more than twenty years later, the danger is still there.

▲ a lot of ash on the slopes of Mount Pinatubo in the Philippines

Comprehension Quiz

A Which of the following does NOT come out of a volcano?

ash

dust

lava

snow

lightning

gas

B Fill in each blank with the right conjunction below.

> and   until   although   but

❶ All lava is dangerous, ______________ there are different types.

❷ Granite is very hard, ______________ it is often used as a building material.

❸ The crust pushes upward ______________, at last, the magma bursts out.

❹ ______________ the crust covers the entire Earth, it is not a solid piece of rock.

 Choose the best answer to each question.

❶ Why is volcanic ash dangerous to human health?

    a) It covers the ground.

    b) It gets into people's lungs.

    c) It blocks the sunlight for a while.

    d) It forms a layer on houses.

❷ Why are the rice fields of the Philippines described as "precious"?

    a) because there is gold in the ground

    b) because people make a lot of money from them

    c) because people cannot eat without them

    d) because people exchange the rice for jewels

D Use the clues and rearrange the letter in the misspelled words so that they are spelled correctly.

❶ PURENIOT – when magma forces its way through the Earth's

    crust onto the surface

❷ TASBAL – a volcanic rock formed when lava cools quickly

❸ HATLEL – a word meaning "deadly"

❹ PIPEOMI – a Roman town buried by volcanic ash

❶_____________   ❷_____________   ❸_____________   ❹_____________

Chapter Two

The Science of Volcanoes

Some scientists say that any volcano that has erupted in the last ten thousand years is active. This may seem like a long time ago, but in terms of volcanic eruptions it's quite recent.

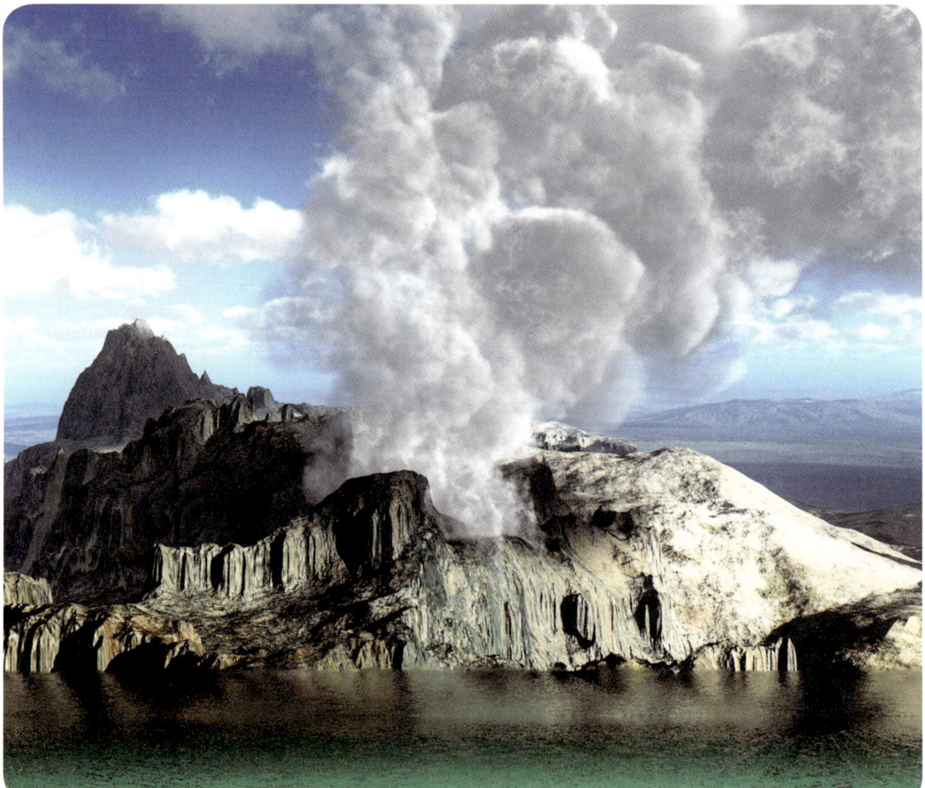

An active volcano is one that has erupted recently, and it may erupt at any time. An eruption may finish quickly, or it may continue for years. In 1943, a volcano erupted in a field near the village of Paricutin, Mexico. It continued to erupt for nine years and 42 days.

A dormant volcano is one that has not erupted for a very long time. It seems to be sleeping. It is quiet, and no lava comes out of it. But it might erupt again one day. Baekdu Mountain, in North Korea, is considered dormant. Hawaii, in the USA, is made up of volcanoes. Two of them are *active*, and the others are *dormant*.

How many active volcanoes are there in Hawaii?

ⓐ 5
ⓑ 2

KEY WORDS

- last
- in terms of
- recent

- active
- at any time
- continue

- dormant
- be considered

Mt. Halla, on Jeju Island in South Korea, is a volcano. It is visited by many people, and it seems to be very quiet. Most people say it is extinct. But since it last erupted a thousand years ago, there are a few scientists that would call it a dormant or even an active volcano.

The problem is that nobody knows when an eruption might happen. There may be warning signs, such as small earthquakes. If scientists think that an eruption may happen soon, they will watch the volcano very closely.

There are thousands of volcanoes around the world that have not erupted for tens of thousands of years. They are not likely to do so again. They are called *extinct* volcanoes. In the UK, Edinburgh Castle is built on top of an extinct volcano.

KEY WORDS

▪ extinct	▪ earthquake	▪ on top of
▪ warning sign	▪ tens of thousands of	▪ solar system
▪ such as	▪ be likely to	▪ hide (hide-hid-hidden)

▲ Edinburgh Castle, built on an extinct volcano

In September 2013, scientists discovered the world's biggest extinct volcano. It is called Tamu Massif. It is one of the biggest volcanoes in the entire solar system and is hidden 2 km beneath the Pacific Ocean.

You might think that all active volcanoes are bad news, yet millions of people still live near them.

For example, the largest active volcano in Europe is Mount Etna on the island of Sicily. It erupts all the time, so ash falls onto gardens and farmland. A lava flow divides two villages. Sometimes it strays too close to buildings and causes damage. Sometimes the airport has to be closed, and earthquakes occur.

Despite all of these problems, one fourth of all the people who live on Sicily choose to live on the slopes of Mount Etna.

Why?

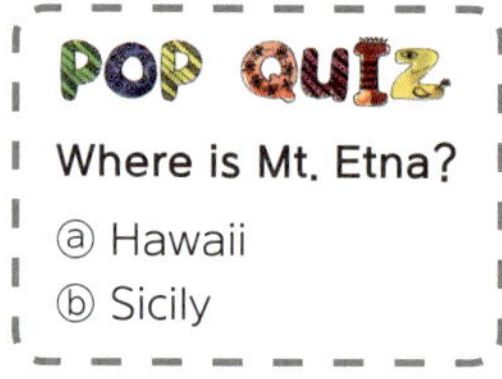

KEY WORDS

- bad news
- all the time
- farmland
- stray

- damage
- despite of
- fertile
- grapevine

- earn money
- agriculture

There are some good things about living near a volcano. The ash that falls onto the ground makes it very fertile. This means that plants grow easily. Grapevines grow especially well in volcanic ash. The people can earn money from agriculture and wine making.

▲ a town on the slopes of Mount Etna

In addition, many tourists visit the island in order to see the volcano. They pay to stay in accommodation and to go on volcano tours. They may like to bathe in hot springs, where the water is naturally heated by the magma far below.

Many different materials can be found near volcanoes. Volcanic rocks are often harder than other types, so they are good for building. They last a long time.

Some archaeologists think that thousands of years ago, humans used volcanic rock to make weapons. Another volcanic material is pumice, a rock that is very light because it is filled with air spaces. 

Some people use pumice to rub hard skin from their feet. They use cosmetics containing pumice to scrub their faces. Pumice can also be made into a powder and added to erasers to rub out pencil marks.

▲ pumice

KEY WORDS

- pumice
- light
- cosmetic
- contain
- scrub
- powder

In some countries, such as Iceland, the heat from the Earth is used to make electricity. This is called geothermal energy. It lights their houses and heats their water, and it won't run out. The Romans were the first to use geothermal energy to heat their homes.

▲ a geothermal energy plant in Iceland

KEY WORDS

- geothermal
- light
- run out
- holy
- sacred
- worship
- prayer

▲ Baekdu Mountain

▲ Mount Fuji

In Japan, Mount Fuji is considered to be a holy mountain. Baekdu Mountain, in Korea, is also sacred to many people. For some people, climbing these volcanoes is a form of worship and prayer. It is certainly true that many volcanic areas are filled with natural beauty. Even those who do not wish to worship go to visit and to enjoy the peace.

Volcanoes are also useful in helping us to learn more about the Earth. Scientists study volcanoes carefully in order to understand what the Earth is like beneath the crust.

But some volcanoes are too dangerous for people to go into, so scientists use small robots to collect data. These robots can go very close to the hot openings where lava is coming out. The heat and the toxic gases do not harm them. They can collect samples of air in order to find out what gases are in it. They can take photographs and record temperatures. In addition, they can travel down steep slopes and over rough surfaces where it would be difficult for humans to walk. They are operated by remote control, so people can stand in safe places and guide the robots.

KEY WORDS

- useful in
- collect
- data
- opening
- harm
- find out
- record
- steep
- rough
- operate
- remote control
- guide

Comprehension Quiz

A Complete the sentences by choosing the correct word.

❶ Tamu Massif is the (biggest / smallest)

volcano on the Earth.

❷ Mt. Etna is an (extinct / active) volcano.

❸ A volcano occurs where two

(villages / plates) meet.

❹ An (earthquake / eruption) is an early

warning sign that a volcano is active.

B Mark T for true or F for false.

❶ There is nothing good about living near a volcano.   T   F

❷ Plants grow well in volcanic ash.   T   F

❸ Tourists stay away from volcanic areas.   T   F

❹ Hot springs are naturally heated by the sun.   T   F

C Choose the best answer to each question.

❶ Where does geothermal energy come from?

a) electricity　　　　　　　b) the sun

c) water　　　　　　　　　d) the earth

❷ How can scientists understand what the Earth is like beneath the crust?

a) by digging a hole

b) by going to the bottom of the sea

c) by studying volcanoes

d) by sending robots down into the mantle

D Rewrite each of the passive sentences in the active form.

❶ A new volcano was discovered by scientists.

→ ____

❷ The island is visited by many tourists.

→ ____

❸ Pumice is used by people to rub hard skin from their feet.

→ ____

Shaking All Over

Volcanoes are not the only things that happen when the plates move on the Earth's crust. Earthquakes happen all of the time.

Some scientists say that each year a million earthquakes occur around the world. About one hundred thousand of them are strong enough to be felt by humans. Not all of them cause damage, but this shows how common earthquakes are.

The worst earthquakes can make buildings fall down. They can crack roads and kill thousands of people. So it is very important that scientists try to understand what causes them. Then, they might be able to predict when a severe earthquake will happen. This could save many lives.

POP QUIZ

Why do scientists want to learn how to predict earthquakes?

ⓐ so that they can collect more data
ⓑ so that they can save people's lives

KEY WORDS

- occur
- common
- **fall down** (fall-fell-fallen)
- crack
- thousands of
- predict
- severe
- save one's life

So what causes an earthquake? Before
the real reason was discovered, different
people in history had ideas about this.
In Japan, people believed that a giant
catfish lived beneath the ground.
When it waved its tail around,
the Earth shook.

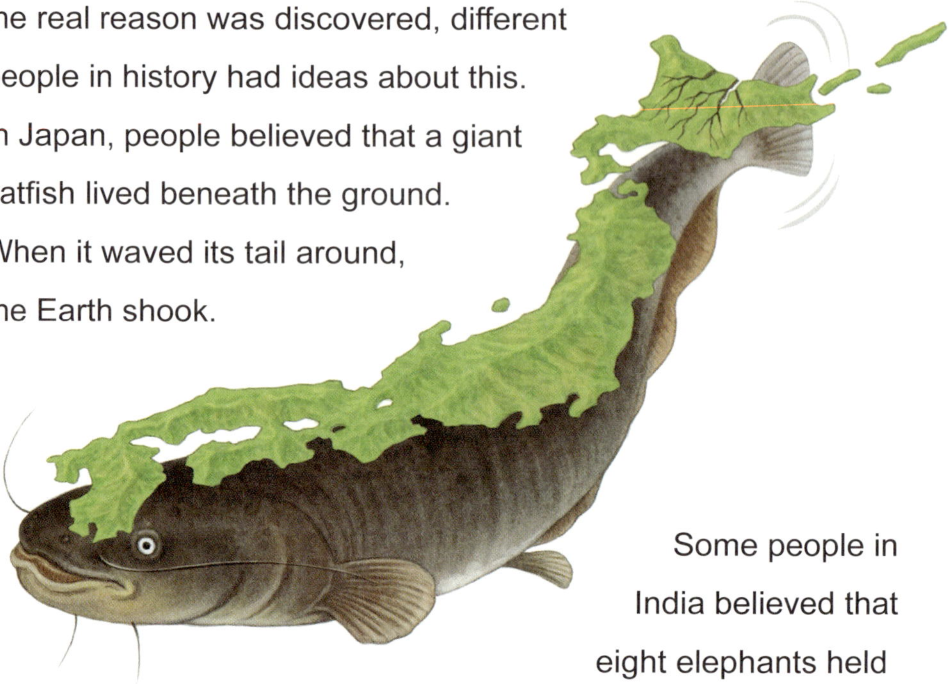

Some people in
India believed that
eight elephants held
up the world. When one
of them got tired and lowered its head, the Earth shook.

Some people in Peru thought that a god
visited the Earth to count how
many people there were.
When this happened,
his footsteps caused
earthquakes.
They ran out of
their houses and
shouted, "I'm here,
I'm here!" They
thought he would
count them and leave
them alone. In fact, running out of
their houses was a very sensible thing to do in case the houses
fell down. 

KEY WORDS

- catfish
- wave
- **hold up** (hold-held-held)
- lower
- leave A alone
- sensible
- in case

But what is the real reason an earthquake happens? Think back to what you already know about the Earth's crust. It is made of separate plates, which are moved about by the convection currents in the mantle. The places where the plates meet are called *fault lines*.

[Why do the earthquakes happen?]

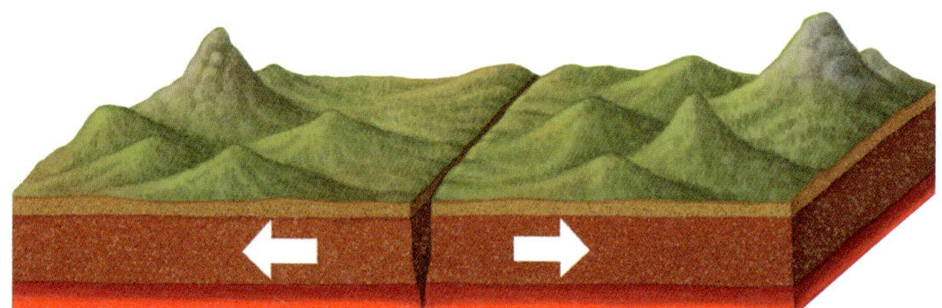

When plates move apart

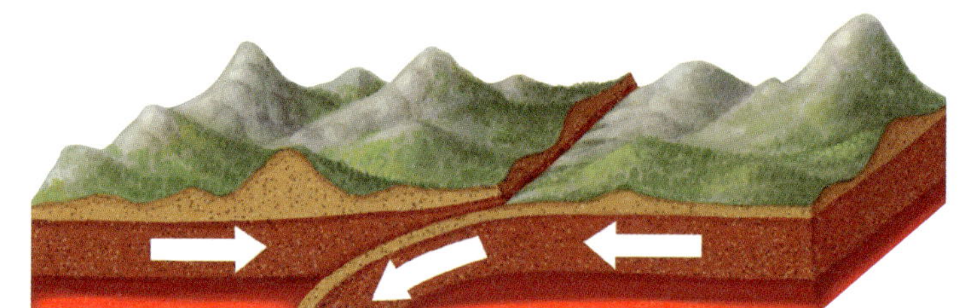

When a piece of one plate is pushed beneath another

When plates scrape against each other

Small earthquakes can happen when plates move apart.
They can also happen when a piece of one plate gets pushed
beneath another. But most earthquakes occur when plates
scrape against each other. If they were smooth, it would not
be a problem. They would glide past each other easily. But
because they are made of rock, they drag against each other.
Often, they get stuck.

An easy way to understand this is to imagine that you are trying
to push past someone in a narrow corridor. At first, you can't get
past even though you might be pushing hard. Suddenly, that
person moves aside, and you fall to the ground. That is what
happens with the plates. The pushing force builds up as they try
to move past each other. Suddenly, one of them gives way, and
the ground shakes.

POP QUIZ

What causes an earthquake?

ⓐ folding of the Earth's crust
ⓑ a movement of plates in the Earth's crust

KEY WORDS

- think back to[on]
- separate
- fault line
- scrape against

- glide
- drag
- get stuck
- narrow

- corridor
- **build up** (build-built-built)
- **give way**

There are fault lines all over the world. Some are short, and some are very long. For example, there are two large fault lines along the coast of Japan. There is also one that runs right through the middle of New Zealand. There are many earthquakes in these countries.

An earthquake hit the New Zealand city of Christchurch in 2010. It damaged two thirds of the homes there. Five months later, another earthquake in the same area killed 185 people.

Choose the correct word or phrase to complete each sentence.

ⓐ There are two large fault lines (away from / along) the coast of Japan.
ⓑ Shock waves travel through the (crust / inner core).

KEY WORDS

- coast
- run through
- **slip** (slip-slipped-slipped)

- shake out
- rug
- shock wave

So why do some earthquakes cause so much damage? When the plates slip past each other, shock waves travel through the crust. It's a bit like someone shaking out a rug. These shock waves shake everything up. The stronger they are, the more damage they do. 

▲ An earthquake hit the New Zealand city of Christchurch in 2010.

The size of an earthquake is measured by using a *seismometer*. This is buried in the ground. It measures the waves that pass through it. It has to be buried very deeply so that it will not shake when heavy trucks pass over it. It measures the strength of the shock waves according to the *Richter Scale*. The Richter Scale is a system of measurement where each value is ten times stronger than the one before.

▲ seismometer

KEY WORDS

- seismometer
- strength
- according to
- Richter Scale
- measurement
- tremor
- tiny

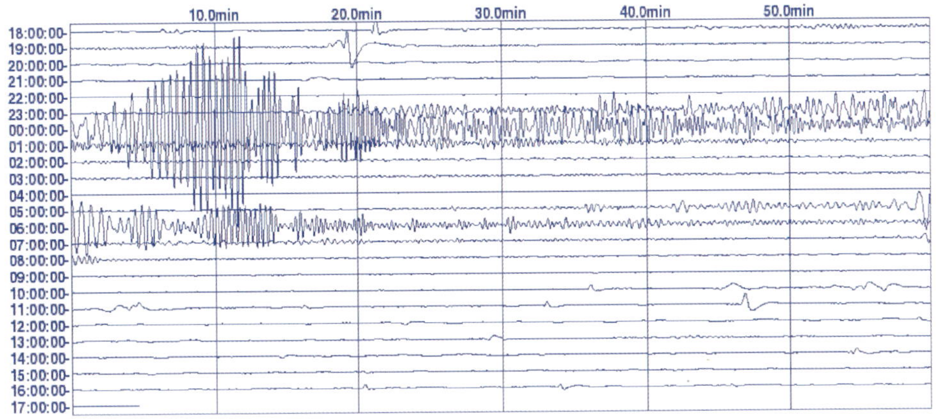

▲ seismogram

For example, an earthquake that measures 1 on the Richter Scale will not be felt by anyone. Such a tiny movement is often called a *tremor*. An earthquake that measures 2 on the Richter Scale is ten times more powerful than a 1. An earthquake that measures 3 is ten times more powerful again. The first earthquake in Christchurch measured 7.1 on the Richter Scale. This means that it was a million times stronger than a tiny 1 tremor!

POP QUIZ

Why does a seismometer need to be buried deep in the ground?

ⓐ so that it won't react to heavy trucks passing overhead
ⓑ so that it can measure earthquakes on the other side
     of the planet

Humans do not notice tremors that are less than 3 on the Richter Scale. At 3, they may hear a low rumble but assume it is a passing truck or thunder. At 4, they may feel some mild shaking. At 5, things may fall off shelves, and the shaking will be felt more strongly. At 6, people may fall over and hurt themselves. Heavy objects such as desks and tables may move. Parts of buildings may crack and fall off. There may be landslides and rockslides that block roads. When the magnitude is 7 or greater, more damage occurs. Buildings collapse, trapping people inside them. The ground cracks, roads twist, and bridges break. Many people are hurt or killed, and thousands more may be left homeless.

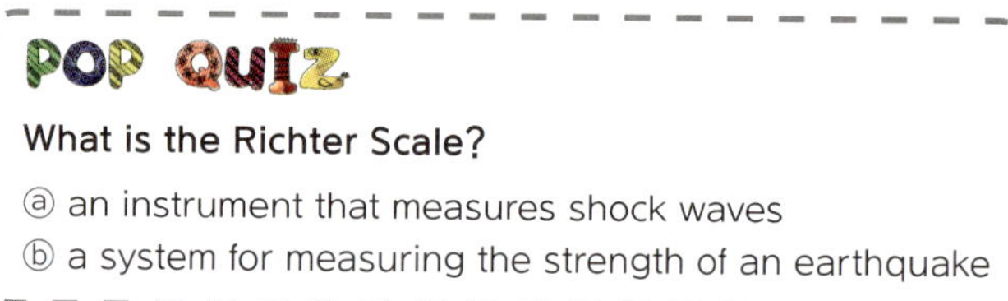

What is the Richter Scale?
ⓐ an instrument that measures shock waves
ⓑ a system for measuring the strength of an earthquake

KEY WORDS

• rumble	• fall over	• magnitude
• assume	• object	• collapse
• fall off	• landslide	• trap
• shelf	• rockslide	• twist

[the Richter Scale and the strength of an earthquake]

There may be even worse problems. If the ground has too much water in it, it turns to liquid. Vehicles and buildings sink into it. When a big earthquake happens beneath the ocean, shock waves travel through the sea. Enormous waves, called *tsunamis*, travel toward land. When they reach land, they wash away people and cars. They break trees and smash through forests and buildings. A famous tsunami happened in December 2004. A huge earthquake happened in the Indian Ocean close to Indonesia. It caused a tsunami, which killed hundreds of thousands of people.

Another earthquake created a tsunami that hit the coast of Japan in 2011. It crushed towns and destroyed families. The people were shocked and frightened, and they are still suffering from the effects.

KEY WORDS

- liquid
- vehicle
- sink (sink-sank-sunk)
- enormous
- wash away
- smash through
- crush
- frightened
- suffer from

Since earthquakes can cause so much damage, it is important that scientists learn how to predict them. There are natural signs that an earthquake might be about to begin. Mild tremors may occur a few days before. This is like a warning that something big is about to happen.

Some people believe that animals know when an earthquake is coming. Frogs and toads leave the water and deep-sea fish rise to the surface. Snakes leave their holes, chickens stop laying eggs, and bees leave their hives. Sometimes dogs bark for no reason, and cats behave strangely.

But scientists need accurate information to predict earthquakes. They need to know when they will happen. They also need to know where they will happen and how big they will be.

This is very difficult to do, and scientists need to be careful. If they say that an earthquake is coming, people will get frightened. They will leave their homes or businesses. If the scientists are wrong and nothing happens, people will be upset. They may even lose money.

KEY WORDS

- be about to
- warning
- toad
- deep-sea
- hive
- behave
- accurate
- upset

So far, nobody has managed to accurately predict a major earthquake. Scientists measure fault lines to see how much they have moved. They look at other earthquakes in order to see if there is a pattern. They study gases within the Earth's crust. In this way, some earthquakes may be predicted. But many still happen without warning.

▲ warning signs for earthquakes and tsunamis

There are some places in the world where scientists believe a large earthquake will occur. The problem is that they don't know when. It could happen tomorrow, or it could happen in a hundred years' time.

KEY WORDS

- so far
- manage to
- major
- look at
- be responsible for
- collapse

One such place is the western coast of the USA. A 1,300 km fault line called the San Andreas Fault runs through California. It was responsible for the great San Francisco earthquake in 1906, when most of the city was destroyed. Buildings collapsed, gas pipes broke, and fires burned for several days. Scientists believe that it could happen again at any time.

▲ The San Andreas Fault runs through California.

In modern cities where earthquakes are common, buildings are designed differently. They sway from side to side in an earthquake instead of collapsing. Some tall buildings have a wide base and are very narrow at the top. This shape is less likely to fall than one which is the same size all the way up.

▲ a building in Japan, designed in case earthquakes happen

But if you ever find yourself in an earthquake, here is some advice from rescue teams around the world.

DROP, COVER, and HOLD ON.

Doing these three things is the best way to keep yourself safe. When an earthquake begins, you should step out of an elevator if you are inside one. Stay in the building and don't go outside. If you have time, turn off any electrical appliances and gas cookers.
This will make things safer for everyone.

POP QUIZ

What type of building is more likely to fall in an earthquake?
ⓐ a building with a wide base and a narrow top
ⓑ a building which is the same size all the way up

KEY WORDS

- sway
- from side to side
- base
- find oneself in
- rescue
- drop
- hold on
- step
- turn off
- electrical appliance
- gas cooker
- things

Drop onto your hands and knees. Then, the shock waves cannot knock you over.

Cover yourself (especially your head) by sheltering under a desk or table.

This way, falling objects are less likely to hurt you. If there is nothing to shelter under, cover your head and neck with your arms.

Hold on to the table, or whatever you are sheltering under, until the shaking stops. If it starts to move about because of the shaking, crawl with it.

In countries where earthquakes are common, school children often practice these things. Then, they are prepared, and they know what to do when a real earthquake happens.

KEY WORDS

- drop onto one's hands and knees
- knock over
- shelter
- crawl
- practice
- prepared

Chapter Three

Comprehension Quiz

A What does each animal do before an earthquake? Match each action with the right animal.

1    • a) bark for no reason

2    • b) stop laying eggs

3    • c) leave the water

4    • d) leave their holes

B Mark T for true or F for false.

1 Earthquakes are very common.   T   F

2 Earthquakes are always dangerous.   T   F

3 Nobody knows what causes an earthquake.   T   F

4 Some earthquakes can make a building fall down.   T   F

C Choose the best answer to each question.

❶ What is the place called where two or more plates meet?

   a) a volcano

   b) an earthquake

   c) a fault line

   d) a mantle

❷ What happens in an earthquake if the ground contains too much liquid?

   a) Buildings sink into the ground.

   b) Tsunamis begin in big cities.

   c) There is a flood.

   d) Nobody gets hurt because the ground is soft.

D The following are the actions you should take when an earthquake happens. Put the sentences in the right order.

❶ Hold onto the table until the earthquake is over.

❷ Drop onto your hands and knees.

❸ Cover yourself by sheltering under a table.

   ________ → _______ → _______

Up in the Air

There is another part of the Earth that isn't joined to it but is still very important. Without it, life on the Earth would not exist. It is the Earth's atmosphere. The atmosphere is the layer of gases around the Earth. Gravity holds it in place. We can't see it, but we can see some of the things that are in it, such as clouds.

KEY WORDS

- exist
- atmosphere
- gravity
- in place
- firstly
- greenhouse effect
- increase
- certain

The atmosphere helps us in many ways. Firstly, it keeps us warm, but not too hot. Light and heat energy from the sun travels through space toward our planet. This energy warms the Earth, and the gases in the atmosphere trap the heat like a giant blanket. This means that our planet is warm enough for life to exist all over it. It never gets too hot during the day or too cold during the night. This effect is called the greenhouse effect. It is a good thing unless there is an increase of certain gases in the atmosphere. Then, the Earth warms up too much. Some scientists believe this is happening today.

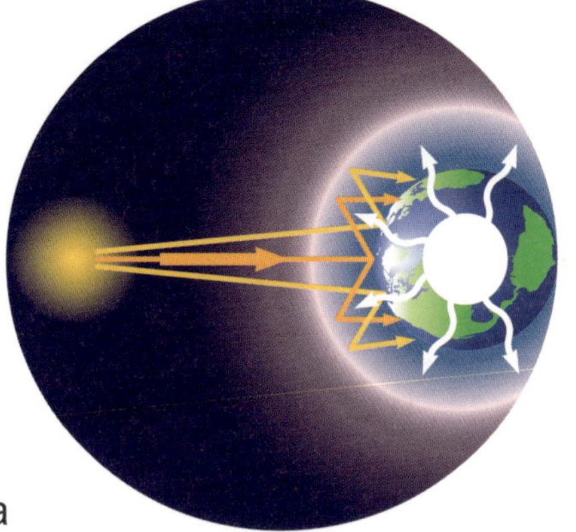

▲ the greenhouse effect

Mark T for true or F for false.

ⓐ The atmosphere is made up of solid layers.　T / F
ⓑ The atmosphere is held in place by gravity.　T / F

Secondly, the atmosphere allows us to breathe. All the gases in the atmosphere together are called air. Human, animals, and plants all need air to survive. Mountaineers who climb very high often notice that they cannot breathe easily. The air there is much thinner because they are high up. (Aha!)

When air moves about in the atmosphere, it makes wind. We can't see it, but we can feel it, we can hear it, and we can see the effect it has on things.

Sometimes you might not feel any wind on the ground. But if you look up, the clouds are moving quickly. This tells you that the wind is blowing higher in the atmosphere.

KEY WORDS

- allow
- survive
- mountaineer
- thin
- effect
- **blow** (blow-blew-blown)

Sometimes, at ground level, the wind is a gentle breeze; sometimes it is a wild hurricane. Scientists measure the force of the wind on a scale of 1 to 12. This is called the Beaufort Scale. Zero means there is no wind at all. 1 to 3 means that there is a light wind, or breeze. The sea is fairly calm, and the wind moves leaves on the trees. This type of wind is very useful. It keeps people cool on a hot day. It dries clothes that have been hung out to dry. It also fills the sails of boats to move them along and allows people to fly kites.

▲ breeze

▲ gale

▲ storm

A wind that reaches 7 or 8 is called a gale. During a gale, trees bend, and twigs may snap off. The sea is rough with high waves and white foam. Tiles may blow off the roofs of houses. People find it difficult to walk against such a strong wind.

When the wind is 10 or 11 on the Beaufort scale, it is called a storm. When this happens, trees are blown down. They can block roads and damage cars. Power lines may also be blown down, so homes lose electricity. Buildings may be damaged, and it can take days for the mess to be cleaned up. The sea is a dangerous place to be in a storm since the waves are incredibly high and ships may tip over.

KEY WORDS

- breeze
- scale
- fairly
- hang out (hang-hung-hung)
- gale
- bend (bend-bent-bent)
- twig
- snap off
- tile
- power line
- mess
- tip over

However, all of these winds are nothing compared with the strength of a force 12 wind. This is known as a hurricane, cyclone or typhoon. These are all the same thing, but they are called by different names depending on where in the world they occur. In Asia, they are generally known as typhoons. In the Atlantic Ocean, they are called hurricanes. Around the Indian Ocean and Australia, people call them cyclones.

Hurricanes are incredibly powerful. The winds move around in a huge circle, which may be several

kilometers across.

Within this circle of wind and clouds, the winds are strong enough to lift cars from the road and throw them through the air. Boats may be snatched from the sea and dumped on a nearby road. Trees blow down, glass windows break, and the air is filled with dirt and garbage.

KEY WORDS

- hurricane
- cyclone
- typhoon
- depend on
- lift
- snatch
- dump
- garbage

The sea is full of massive waves, which may break over the beach and flood large areas. People must take shelter or leave an area completely while a hurricane lasts. This may take several hours or even days.

KEY WORDS

- massive
- break over
- take shelter
- completely
- swirling
- alternately
- flood
- inland

In the very center of the swirling circle of winds is an area called the eye of the hurricane. Here, it is completely calm. It may feel as though the danger has passed,  but as the eye moves on, the strong winds start again.

▲ the eye of the hurricane

Hurricanes are such powerful things that scientists give each one a name. They are given a male name and a female name alternately, according to the letters of the alphabet. Perhaps one of the most famous hurricanes of the 21st century was Hurricane Katrina, which hit the American city of New Orleans in 2005. 80% of the city was flooded with sea water reaching up to 19 km inland from the coast.

The floodwater stayed in the streets for many weeks. It left people trapped in their homes with no power, food, or fresh water to drink. More than 1,800 people died, and thousands were left homeless.

The most powerful typhoon ever recorded was Typhoon Haiyan. The wind speed was around 315 kph at its strongest. It hit the Philippines in November 2013 and devastated large areas. It is estimated that ten million people were affected. Hundreds of people were killed, and many others were left homeless, without food or water. A national calamity was declared by the Government and other countries sent aid to help them.

▲ Typhoon Haiyan hit the Philippines in 2013.

Another dangerous type of wind is a tornado. A tornado is a column of air that is spinning around. The top end is joined to a storm cloud, and the bottom end touches the ground. Normally, you cannot see air, but a tornado may be full of water droplets and dust. It looks like a dark, twisting tube that travels quickly across the ground. There are thousands of tornadoes every year. Most of them are small and only travel a few kilometers before they disappear.

But sometimes things are very different. A violent tornado struck the American state of Oklahoma in May 2013. It was several kilometers across and continued for 39 minutes. During that time, it traveled 27 km through a city neighborhood. It destroyed houses, schools, and hospitals, and it killed and injured many people.

POP QUIZ

If air is invisible, why can tornadoes easily be seen?
ⓐ They are full of water droplets and dust.
ⓑ They are full of dirt and garbage.

KEY WORDS

- tornado
- column
- spin
- storm cloud

- droplet
- tube
- violent
- **strike** (strike-struck-striken)

- continue
- neighborhood
- injure

There are many ways in which the Earth reminds us of its power. Earthquakes, volcanoes, and strong winds show us that the Earth is never still. It is moving and changing all of the time.
It is a restless Earth.

KEY WORDS

- remind
- still
- restless

Comprehension Quiz

A Match the two sides.

1

breeze

2

gale

3

storm

4

hurricane

a) Trees bend.

b) Power lines blow down.

c) Clothes dry.

d) Cars fly through the air.

B Fill in each blank with the right word below.

leaves	sails	waves	tiles

1 ______________ may blow off the roofs of houses.

2 ______________ may move on the trees.

3 ______________ may fill with wind and move boats along.

4 ______________ may become high and foamy.

 Choose the best answer to each question.

❶ What is the best description of wind?

a) a gas in the atmosphere

b) air moving through the atmosphere

c) energy from space

d) a form of cloud

❷ Which of the statements below is true of hurricanes, typhoons, and cyclones?

a) They only occur over land.

b) They are all below 10 on the Beaufort Scale.

c) They are all given a name.

d) They rarely cause damage.

D Put the sentences about "the greenhouse effect" in the right order.

❶ The gases in the atmosphere trap the warmth.

❷ The sun's energy reaches the Earth.

❸ The sun's energy warms the Earth.

❹ The Earth stays at just the right temperature.

__________ → __________ → __________ → __________

Let's Review the Story

Fill in the blanks to review the story.

❶ Title: ____________

❷ Main Idea: There are natural events on the __________ that cause d __________ and d __________ .

❸ Introduction: The Earth has four layers: the __________ , the __________ , the __________ , and the __________ .

❹ Natural Event 1 – __________

These may be e __________ , d __________ , or a __________ .
An e __________ occurs when l __________ , g __________ , and a __________ come out.

Natural Event 2 – __________

These occur when two p __________ slip past each other.
The s __________ w __________ in the c __________ can make b __________ fall down.

Natural Event 3 – Strong __________

These include t __________ , h __________ , c __________ , and t __________ .

❺ Summary : From __________ , the Earth looks c __________ . In reality, it is r __________ and d __________ .

Think about the following questions and answer them freely.

❶ Like ancient people did, imagine the Earth were hollow so that you could explore inside. Tell us what kind of adventure you'd want to have inside it.

❷ Tell us what actions you should take if an earthquake occurs and how buildings should be built so that they won't collapse.

❸ If there were no air surrounding the Earth, imagine how different the world would be.

❹ Explain what happens during a hurricane.

Let's Review the Story

❶ **Title:** Restless Earth

❷ **Main Idea:** There are natural events on the Earth that cause damage and destruction.

❸ **Introduction:** The Earth has four layers: the crust, the mantle, the outer core, and the inner core.

❹ **Natural Event 1 –** Volcanoes

These may be extinct, dormant, or active.

An eruption occurs when lava, gas, and ash come out.

Natural Event 2 – Earthquakes

These occur when two plates slip past each other.

The shock waves in the crust can make buildings fall down.

Natural Event 3 – Strong winds

These include typhoons, hurricanes, cyclones, and tornadoes.

❺ **Summary :** From space, the Earth looks calm. In reality, it is restless and dangerous.

- Restless Earth
- Level 5
- 27 Questions

(Vocabulary 5 / Reading Comprehension 16 /

Sentence Structure & Grammar 6)

1. Which of the following has the closest meaning with the word "fragile"?
   ① peaceful   ② smooth
   ③ delicate   ④ calm

2. Which of the following has the closest meaning with the word "toxic"?
   ① boiling   ② dangerous
   ③ quick   ④ poisonous

3. Which of the following has the opposite meaning with the word "massive"?
   ① tiny
   ② huge
   ③ enormous
   ④ large

※ Choose the common word for the two blanks. (4~5)

4.
   • The mantle is also ___________ of rock.
   • An enormous onion is ___________ up of different layers.

   ① taken   ② got
   ③ made   ④ moved

5.
   • This type of wind keeps people ___________ on a hot day.
   • Magma hits the cold seawater, and ___________s to solid rock.

   ① hot   ② hard
   ③ smooth   ④ cool

6. Which of the following sentences best describes the Earth's crust?
    ① It is completely flat and is made of rock.
    ② It is flat in some places and folded in others.
    ③ It is underwater and is folded everywhere.
    ④ It is one solid piece of rock.

7. Why was it a good thing if some people ran out of their houses during an
    earthquake?
    ① They could measure the strength of the earthquake.
    ② They would be safe if their houses fell down.
    ③ They could make sure their animals were safe.
    ④ They could count each other.

8. Which of the following is NOT an effect of a tsunami?
    ① People and cars are washed away.
    ② Trees are broken.
    ③ Buildings are smashed.
    ④ Fires are started in forests.

9. Why is the atmosphere described as "a blanket"?
    ① because it is very thick
    ② because it lets energy pass through it
    ③ because it keeps us warm
    ④ because it is made of a single layer

10. Why can't mountaineers who climb very high breathe well?
    ① They have done too much exercise.
    ② They are carrying heavy loads.
    ③ The mountain air gives them lung diseases.
    ④ The air gets thinner as they climb high.

11. Why is it dangerous to be on a boat during a hurricane? Choose two answers.
   ① The people on board have no shelter from the rain.
   ② The high waves might tip the boat over.
   ③ The boat may be thrown onto dry land.
   ④ The boat may go around in circles.

12. Why could life on the Earth NOT exist without the atmosphere? Choose two answers.
   ① The Earth would be either too hot or too cold.
   ② The sun's energy would not reach the Earth.
   ③ There would be no air to breathe on the Earth.
   ④ There would be no gravity to keep people and animals on the Earth.

13. Which of the following is NOT a method of predicting an earthquake?
   ① studying the gases within the Earth's crust
   ② measuring fault lines to see how much they have moved
   ③ measuring how much buildings sway from side to side
   ④ looking at other earthquakes to see if there is a pattern

14. An earthquake measures 2 on the Richter Scale. A second earthquake measures 5 on the Richter Scale. How many times stronger is the second earthquake than the first?
   ① 10 times stronger
   ② 100 times stronger
   ③ 1,000 times stronger
   ④ 10,000 times stronger

15. Which is a warning sign that a volcanic eruption might occur soon?
   ① the presence of hot springs
   ② a small earthquake
   ③ ash falling from the sky
   ④ a sudden increase in air temperature

16. Why might the people of the Philippines fear heavy rain?
   ① It turns volcanic ash into deadly mud flows.
   ② They cannot go outside when it is raining.
   ③ It floods their rice fields.
   ④ It stops the rice from growing.

17. In 2010, why did many European airports close when a volcano erupted in Iceland?
   ① It was too dark for aircraft to fly.
   ② There was too much lightning for aircraft to fly.
   ③ The ash could have damaged the aircraft engines.
   ④ There was lava on the runways.

18. After Hurricane Katrina, why did the people of New Orleans have no water to drink?
   ① There was no water anywhere in the city.
   ② There was plenty of floodwater, but none of it was clean.
   ③ They had left their homes without taking any water with them.
   ④ They lived a long way from rivers and the sea.

19. What is the main advantage of geothermal energy over other types of energy?
   ① It makes electricity.
   ② It won't run out.
   ③ It heats water.
   ④ It was first used by the Romans.

20. What type of crop grows especially well in volcanic ash?
   ① wheat   ② corn
   ③ grapes   ④ rice

21. Which of these statements is true about both Mt. Fuji and Baekdu Mountain?

① They are extinct volcanoes.

② They are sacred to some people.

③ They are closed to tourists.

④ They erupt regularly.

※ Choose the wrong part of each sentence. (22~23)

22.
If two <u>plates</u> are pulled <u>apart</u>, a gap <u>appears</u> <u>among</u> them.
      ①   ②   ③   ④

23.
The <u>strong</u> they <u>are</u>, the <u>more</u> <u>damage</u> they do.
  ①   ②   ③   ④

※ Choose the correct word for each blank. (24~25)

24.
It was __________ dangerous to fly aircraft because the ash could get into the engines.

① too   ② to

③ much   ④ many

25.
Have you ever __________ exactly what is beneath your feet?

① wondering   ② wonder

③ wondered   ④ wonderance

26. ① Run out of their houses was a very sensible thing to do in case the houses fell down.

② Ran out of their houses was a very sensible thing to do in case the houses fell down.

③ Runner out of their houses was a very sensible thing to do in case the houses fell down.

④ Running out of their houses was a very sensible thing to do in case the houses fell down.

27. ① The Richter Scale is a system of measurement where each value is ten stronger than the one before.

② The Richter Scale is a system of measurement where each value is ten times stronger than the one before.

③ The Richter Scale is a system of measurement where each value is ten times strong as the one before.

④ The Richter Scale is a system of measurement where each value is as ten times stronger than the one before.

Sarah J. Dodd
Sarah J. Dodd is an experienced primary school teacher who resides in the UK, but has also taught in Australia.
She has a PhD in Science and a certificate in Creative Writing. She has published four books for younger children
— 'An Angel Anyway' (Anyway Press) and the Little Angels' series (Lion Hudson plc). Her children's Bible will be
published in 2015. She is currently working on a novel for 9-12 year olds and another for young adults.

Smart Readers
Wise & Wide 5-2

Restless Earth

Written by Sarah J. Dodd
Illustrated by Sangjeong Sim

First Published in December 2014

Editorial Manager: Juyon Choi
Editors: Juyon Choi, Jeeyoung Kim, Kyunghee Jang, Jiyeong Park
Designer: Eunhee Lee
Cover Designer: Eunhee Lee

Published and distributed by

Happy House

Darakwon Bldg., 64-1 Jandari-ro, Mapo-gu, Seoul, Korea 121-894
Tel: 82-2-736-2031(ext. 250)   Fax: 82-2-736-2037
Homepage: www.ihappyhouse.co.kr
Publisher: Kyudo Chung

ISBN: 978-89-6653-167-7 18740 / 978-89-6653-156-1 18740(set)

[Components]
• 1 Audio CD (Recording Studio: Aram)
• Answer Keys & Korean Translation: Free download at www.ihappyhouse.co.kr